Pebble® Plus

Investigate the Seasons

Let's Look at Autumn

Revised Edition

Sarah L Schuette

raintree

a Capstone company — publishers for children

Raintree is an imprint of Capstone Global Library Limited, a company incorporated in England and Wales having its registered office at 264 Banbury Road, Oxford, OX2 7DY – Registered company number: 6695582

www.raintree.co.uk
myorders@raintree.co.uk

Editorial credits
Sarah Bennett, designer; Tracy Cummins, media researcher, Laura Manthe, production specialist

Photo credits
Shutterstock: Dave Allen Photography, 7, DmZ, 5, Erik Mandre, 15, FotoRequest, 13, Grisha Bruev, 9, images72, 17, Liubou Yasiukovich, Cover Design Element, Manamana, 11, Nancy Gill, 19, nikitsin. smugmug.com, 1, Piotr Krzeslak, Cover, Sofiaworld, 3, Victor Grow, 21

Printed and bound in India

ISBN 978 1 4747 5662 4
22 21 20 19 18
10 9 8 7 6 5 4 3 2 1

British Library Cataloguing in Publication Data
A full catalogue record for this book is available from the British Library.

Contents

It's autumn!

How do you know it's autumn?

A cool breeze blows.

The weather is colder.

4

Leaves change colour.

They flutter to the ground.

The sun sets earlier.

Autumn days are shorter

than summer days.

9

Animals in autumn

What do animals do

in autumn?

Squirrels rush around.

They gather nuts

to store for winter.

Birds fly south.

They look

for warmer weather.

Bears search for a place

to hibernate.

Their fur coats grow thicker.

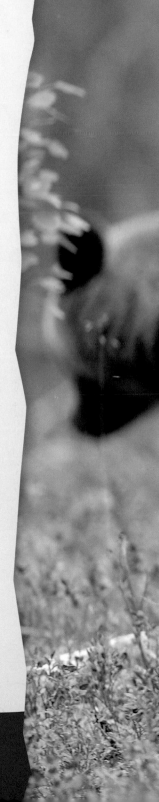

Plants in autumn

What happens

to plants in autumn?

Ripe apples fill the orchard.

They're ready to be picked.

Corn ripens in the field.

It's ready to be harvested.

What's next?

The temperature grows cold.

Autumn is over.

What season is next?

Glossary

breeze gentle wind

flutter wave, flap or float in a breeze; leaves flutter as they drop off tree branches

harvest gather crops that are ready to be picked; autumn is a time for harvesting crops such as corn, soybeans, wheat and oats

hibernate spend the winter in a deep sleep

orchard field or farm where fruit trees grow

ripen become ready to be picked

season one of the four parts of the year; winter, spring, summer and autumn are seasons

weather condition outdoors at a certain time and place; weather changes with each season

Find out more

Books

Autumn (Seasons), Stephanie Turnbull (Franklin Watts, 2015)

Seasons (Ways into Science), Peter Riley (Franklin Watts, 2016)

What Can You See in Autumn? (Seasons), Sian Smith (Raintree, 2014)

Websites

www.dkfindout.com/uk/earth/seasons
Learn more about the seasons on this website.

www.bbc.co.uk/nature/collections/p00bdxqw
Enjoy some autumn videos!

Comprehension questions

1. Describe two signs that it is autumn.

2. What do squirrels do in autumn?

3. Describe what "harvest" means. Use the glossary to help you.

Index